EXPLORING

Landmarks

Seaside Towns

Danielle Sensier and Amanda Earl

WAYLAND

Landmarks

EXPLORING **Inner Cities**
EXPLORING **Seaside Towns**
EXPLORING **Suburbs**
EXPLORING **Villages**

Cover: The famous Tower at Blackpool, in Lancashire (main picture), donkey rides on Skegness beach (top), and a young girl having fun at the seaside.
Title page: The town of Salcombe, in South Devon, is popular with British families because of its safe, sandy beaches and good climate.
Contents page: The harbour at Ilfracombe, in North Devon.

Series editor: Katie Orchard
Book editor: Louise Woods
Designers: Tim Mayer and Malcolm Walker
Production controller: Carol Stevens
Consultant: Rob Unwin, Development Education Centre, Sheffield

First published in 1997 by Wayland Publishers Ltd
61 Western Road, Hove
East Sussex, BN3 1JD, England

British Library Cataloguing in Publication Data
Earl, Amanda
   Seaside towns. – (Landmarks)
   1. Cities and towns – Juvenile literature 2. Seaside architecture - Juvenile literature
   I. Title II. Sensier, Danielle
307. 7 ' 6 ' 09146
ISBN 0 7502 1883 5

Typeset by Mayer Media
Printed and bound in Italy by G. Canale S.p.A.

Picture acknowledgements:
Charles Barker plc: 36 (bottom); Jennie Chapman: 11 (top), 21 (bottom), 22 (bottom), 25; Essex County Council, David Bartam: 24 (top); Eye Ubiquitous: 14 (top), 22 (top), 34 (top), 40/ A J G Bell 33 (top)/ Davy Bold 28/ Davey Boyle 23/ Sylvia Greenland 13/ Stephen Rafferty 18 (top)/ Paul Thompson *cover* (top and main pictures), *contents page*, 4 (top), 32, 37 (bottom); Pat and Martin Fitzgerald: 19 (both); Phil Holden: 36 (top); Impact Photos: Alan Blair 15, 35/ Mark Cator 8/ Piers Cavendish *title page*, 38/ Stuart Clarke 33 (bottom)/ Michael Good 5/ Chris Moyse 34 (bottom)/ Tony Page 10, 16 (top)/ David Reed 4 (bottom), 39/ Roger Scrutton 31/ Simon Shepheard 6/ Homer Sykes 12, 14 (bottom), 16 (bottom)/Francesca Yorke 20 (both); *Isle of White County Press*: 41; *The Lowestoft Journal*: 17; The Mayflower County Primary School, Harwich: 24 (bottom); Mary Evans Picture Library: 11 (bottom), 13; Public Records Office: 30 (top); St Luke's Junior School, Brighton: 26 (both); Mark Smales: 9 (both); Paul Tavener: 29 (top); Trinity House: 29 (bottom); Wayland Picture Library: 18 (bottom), 21 (top)), 21(top), 30 (bottom); Zefa *cover* (left). The artwork on pages7, 10, 27, 43 and 47 is by Peter Bull.

Contents

What is a Seaside Town?   4

People and Communities   8

Earning a Living   16

Seaside Schools   24

On the Move   28

Shopping and Entertainment   32

Planning for the Future   38

How to Investigate a Seaside Town   42

Notes About this Book   44

Glossary   46

Books To Read   47

Index   48

What is a Seaside Town?

There is more to a seaside town than buckets and spades, and a trip to the pier. Seaside towns are also places where people live and work. They are coastal settlements.

The UK has 15,000 kilometres of coastline. This means that there are many seaside towns, from small fishing ports such as Mousehole, in Cornwall and Ardglass in County Down, Northern Ireland, to large holiday towns or resorts, such as Blackpool, in Lancashire and Great Yarmouth, in Norfolk.

Above The old fishing port of Brixham, in Devon, is popular with visitors.

Left Many seaside towns are in 'Areas of Outstanding Natural Beauty'. The Giant's Causeway near Portrush, in County Antrim, Northern Ireland, is a natural landmark made up of 38,000 stone columns.

You can find seaside towns all along the coast, and they all have different natural features. Many of the oldest seaside towns used to be small fishing ports or naval bases, built around safe natural harbours or on estuaries. Some seaside towns are found on headlands, with narrow streets running down to the sea, such as Whitby, in North Yorkshire. Others have dramatic natural features which are also important landmarks, such as the famous 'white cliffs' of Dover, in Kent. Many seaside towns are popular with holidaymakers because of their sandy beaches and sheltered bays, while others have long pebble beaches.

SEASIDE POPULATIONS

Town	Resident Population
Ardglass, County Down	1,700
Lyme Regis, Dorset	3,500
St Ives, Cornwall	10,000
St Andrews, Fife	11,500
Skegness, Lincolnshire	16,000
Poole, Dorset	138,000

Portobello beach near Edinburgh, in Scotland. The wooden groynes are breakwaters which control the movement of sand and pebbles along the beach.

Artificial features, such as piers and lighthouses, are also important landmarks to look out for in a seaside town. Old stone harbours provide a safe place for fishing boats. Modern marinas have been built to house large luxury yachts and small sailing boats. Bridges help people to get around towns situated on estuaries, linking one part of the town to the other. Cowes, on the Isle of Wight, has an unusual floating bridge over the River Medina, connecting it with East Cowes.

RAINFALL AND SUNSHINE

In the north and west of the UK, there is more rainfall than in other areas:

Rainfall in June 1996 (mm)

Eskdalemuir (W.Scotland)	86	Bognor Regis (S.England)	19

In the south and east, there is more sunshine:

Sunshine in June 1996 (hours per day)

Eskdalemuir	6.7	Bognor Regis	10.1

A seaside pier is a prominent landmark which can be seen from all around. Can you spot the helter-skelter ride on this one, in Brighton?

As seaside towns developed into holiday resorts, large piers and promenades were built to entertain all the new visitors. These artificial features are attractive landmarks and are always popular with holidaymakers.

Climate

The climate makes a difference to the popularity of seaside resorts. In the summer, the south and east coasts of the UK have more sunshine than other areas. But the overall climate of the UK is variable, which means that the weather can change quickly from day to day. Nowadays many people travel abroad for their holidays in search of warmer weather. To encourage them to stay in the UK, indoor leisure attractions are now being built all over the UK, which people can visit all year round.

Activity

Imagine you are on holiday in Scarborough. Use the map to plan an exciting weekend of activities for you and your family.

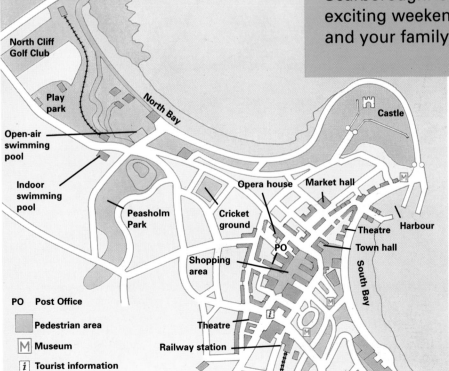

This map of Scarborough shows some of the exciting activities that you can do there.

Sea life centre

North Cliff Golf Club

Play park

North Bay

Castle

Open-air swimming pool

Indoor swimming pool

Opera house   Market hall

Peasholm Park

Cricket ground

Theatre   Harbour

PO

Town hall

Shopping area

South Bay

PO   Post Office

Pedestrian area

M   Museum

Theatre

i   Tourist information

Railway station

People and Communities

Newquay, in Cornwall, has been popular with tourists since Victorian times. Today's holidaymakers enjoy exploring its old streets and buildings.

Whehen you look at a lively seaside town crowded with holidaymakers, it is difficult to imagine what it was like before it became a large resort. But if you visit the old buildings and look at old photographs and postcards, you will find out about the town's development over the years.

Early years

Most seaside towns were originally small fishing villages. The sea was all-important, providing fish to eat and sell. Some seaside towns have old fishermen's cottages that are still lived in today.

Flamborough Lifeboat Crew

For over 170 years, the crews of the Royal National Lifeboat Institute (RNLI) have watched over the coasts of the UK, rescuing people stranded at sea. Today, there are lifeboat stations in most seaside towns.

Christopher Hoskison has been Captain of the Flamborough Lifeboat station for four years. Christopher is in charge of a crew of sixteen — twelve men and four women. The crew members do not get paid and all of them have other jobs.

The crew members each carry a bleeper. When it goes off, they have to race to the station as quickly as possible. The first three crew members to arrive at the station go out on the rescue.

Apart from the crew, there are five tractor drivers who push the boat on its special carriage into the sea.

'In 1995 we made forty-four rescues and saved eight lives,' says Christopher.

Above **Christopher Hoskison (centre) and his crew.**

Below **The Flamborough crew uses an Atlantic 75 Inshore Lifeboat – a fast rescue boat equipped to go out in the most terrible storms.**

Some coastal settlements became important defence posts because of their position overlooking the sea. From Norman times, castles and look-out towers were built along the south-east coast of England to defend it against European invasion.

Other settlements were important to the Navy. The location of Harwich, on the North Sea in Essex, has made it an important naval town for hundreds of years.

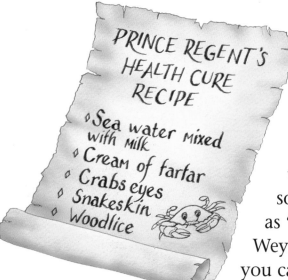

PRINCE REGENT'S HEALTH CURE RECIPE

◊ Sea water mixed with milk
◊ Cream of tartar
◊ Crabs eyes
◊ Snakeskin
◊ Woodlice

Sea cures

It only became popular to visit seaside towns in the eighteenth century, when they were made fashionable by the Prince Regent. At this time, many people believed that drinking sea water was good for your health. Until Victorian times, people did not swim in the sea, but were sometimes dipped in it by special servants known as 'dippers'. Rich people flocked to towns such as Weymouth, in Dorset and Brighton, in Sussex, where you can still see beautiful Regency houses built in grand squares and sweeping crescents.

This is a typical Regency seaside terrace in Brighton. Can you see the bay windows, the balconies and the columns at the doorways?

Above Bathing machines at Brighton's West Pier in Victorian times, lined up and ready for action.

Right A Regency cartoon, showing Scarborough's famous 'dipper' – Widow Ducker.

Later, during Victorian times, seaside towns became popular holiday resorts. People went to the seaside to enjoy the fresh air, walk on the promenade or go for a swim. But going swimming was very different in those days. Swimmers were pulled out to sea by horse-drawn bathing machines. Men and women had to use separate beaches or swim at different times, and they wore dark, heavy swimming costumes which covered them from head to toe!

Every year, thousands of people visit this Bournemouth park to listen to open-air concerts.

The importance of the railways

Before the 1800s, seaside towns were only visited by wealthy people. The introduction of the railways in the 1840s changed all this for good. As railway tracks spread across the country, it became easier for people to visit the seaside. Many more seaside towns developed into holiday resorts, which grew quickly. If you visit the seaside today, you can see many features that were built during the nineteenth century. Look out for piers, promenades, large hotels and bandstands. Many of these are still being used.

	Resident population	Summer population
Poole, Dorset	138,000	Over 2 million
Portrush, County Antrim	5,000	25,000

Different seasons

Some people in seaside towns live there all the time. They are called the resident population. What makes a seaside town different from other settlements is that during the summer months thousands of people visit the seaside. Visitors to seaside towns provide a lot of employment for the residents, but these jobs only last for the summer season. Small hotels and shops often have to make enough money in the summer to last the whole year through. In small seaside towns, such as Tenby in Wales, many of the shops, cafés and amusements close down completely for the winter.

What's in a name?

The name of a seaside town can give you a clue as to how and why it has developed. Some names show the age of the town, such as Scarborough, named after the tenth-century Viking, Thorgils Skarthi. Towns such as Lyme Regis and Bognor Regis are named after royal people who stayed there ('Regis' means 'belonging to a king'). Some names have a military history – Harwich comes from 'here' meaning 'army', and 'wic' meaning 'camp'.

Lyme Regis was popular with royalty in the eighteenth and nineteenth centuries, so 'Regis' was added to its name.

Above The town of Aberystwyth, in Dyfed, in Wales, is hemmed in by the sea on one side and by beautiful hills on the other.

Below The warm climate of seaside towns, such as Bournemouth, has always attracted retired people.

Seaside homes

If you look around a seaside town, you will see modern houses and blocks of flats as well as old Victorian terraces. The older homes are likely to be in the centre of the town and near the seafront. Newer houses have usually been built round them.

It is often difficult for planners to find space for new buildings because the coastline stops any development towards the sea, and the countryside is often protected to stop any building inland. So many towns develop along a narrow strip of coastline.

One solution is to build high-rise flats. Many seaside towns have blocks of flats with balconies looking out to sea. As many older people like to retire by the seaside, there are also rest homes and retirement flats.

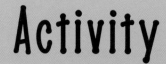

Many of the grand Regency terraces, which were once large single houses, have now been divided into small flats. Some of these are luxury apartments, while others are cramped and have shared bathrooms. In popular resorts, landlords can charge high rents, and house prices are also high. This makes it difficult for people on a low income to find a home.

Living by the sea has other problems. Houses near the sea may flood in bad weather, and sea winds and salty air attack the walls and paintwork of buildings. Seaside communities are also concerned about the pollution of the sea, and the problem of litter on land. Litter is dangerous to wildlife and bad for tourism.

Activity

Every kind of settlement has its own good and bad features. Think about where you live, and make up a list of its problems and attractions. How do they compare?

In winter, strong winds and rough seas keep people away from the Scarborough seafront. Bad weather conditions can sometimes cause heavy flooding.

WARNING
IT IS DANGEROUS
TO BATHE IN
THIS PART OF THE

Earning a Living

People who live in seaside towns often have jobs that are nothing to do with the sea. Like everyone else in the UK, many people work in service industries, such as shops, offices, schools, libraries and hospitals.

Living from the sea

About 250 years ago, the sea provided nearly all the work for people at the seaside, and almost every family was involved in fishing or sailing.

Above Many fishing boats are now used to take tourists on day trips.

Below A traditional wooden boat being built.

Over the centuries, the fishing industry grew from just a few fishermen to an industry employing many thousands of people, but now it is declining.

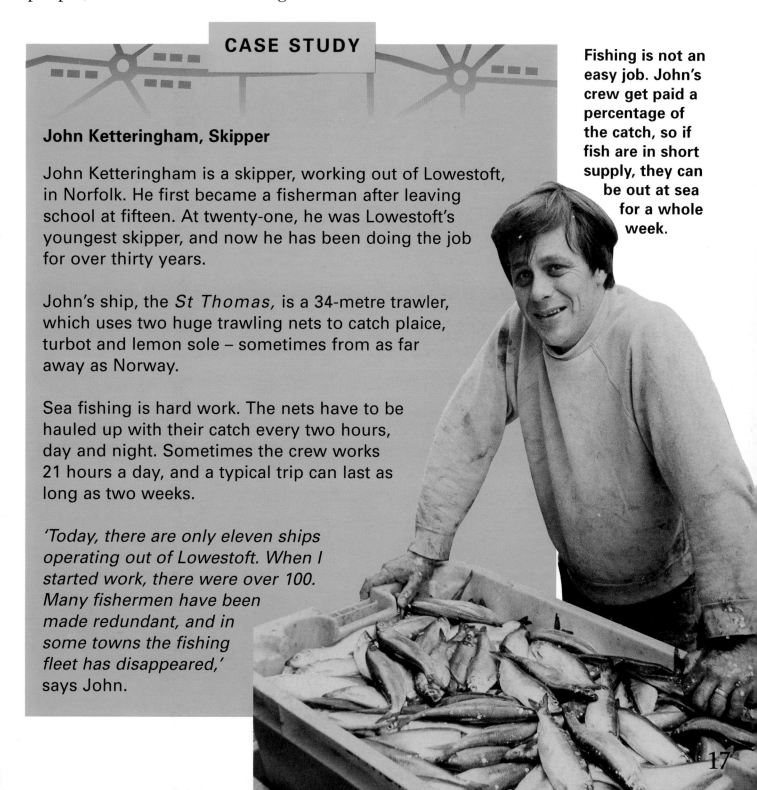

CASE STUDY

John Ketteringham, Skipper

John Ketteringham is a skipper, working out of Lowestoft, in Norfolk. He first became a fisherman after leaving school at fifteen. At twenty-one, he was Lowestoft's youngest skipper, and now he has been doing the job for over thirty years.

John's ship, the *St Thomas,* is a 34-metre trawler, which uses two huge trawling nets to catch plaice, turbot and lemon sole – sometimes from as far away as Norway.

Sea fishing is hard work. The nets have to be hauled up with their catch every two hours, day and night. Sometimes the crew works 21 hours a day, and a typical trip can last as long as two weeks.

'Today, there are only eleven ships operating out of Lowestoft. When I started work, there were over 100. Many fishermen have been made redundant, and in some towns the fishing fleet has disappeared,' says John.

Fishing is not an easy job. John's crew get paid a percentage of the catch, so if fish are in short supply, they can be out at sea for a whole week.

17

The growth of tourism

When seaside towns became holiday resorts, new jobs were created, providing different kinds of work on the piers and promenades, as well as in the hotels and shops. Entertainers of every kind were in demand, and the towns attracted musicians, actors and street entertainers.

Temporary work

Waiters, chambermaids, pier workers, lifeguards and deckchair attendants usually have temporary jobs. Other kinds of work are sometimes temporary, too. In Mablethorpe in Lincolnshire, there are so few visitors out of season, that the traffic wardens are employed only in the summer!

Above Many lifeguards only work for a few months a year – their work is seasonal.

Right Chambermaids have to make hundreds of beds in the summer season.

18

The Trevelyan Hotel, Penzance

Pat and Martin Fitzgerald have run the Trevelyan Hotel in Penzance for twelve years. It is an eighteenth-century building in one of the most historic parts of the town and only two minutes' walk from the sea. Some walkers and cyclists visit the hotel on their way from Land's End to John O'Groats.

The Trevelyan is a small, family-run business. There are eight bedrooms, and guests pay a set price for 'bed and breakfast'. It is only in the busy summer season that a temporary chambermaid is employed.

Every morning, Pat gets up early to cook breakfast for her guests.

'A traditional English breakfast of bacon and eggs is still very popular. We must get through more than 4,500 eggs a year!' says Pat.

Above Although the Trevelyan Hotel is busiest in the summer, it is open all year round. This is because there is so much to see and do in this part of Cornwall in all seasons.

Right Pat and Martin have to work every day that the hotel is open, and that means seven days a week.

Unemployment

Over the last thirty years, the economic situation of most seaside towns has become worse. This is partly because of a decline in the national economy, and partly because seaside towns have often depended too much on tourism.

In a seaside town, fewer tourists means fewer jobs, and without other work to fall back on, unemployment is a problem. Local people often have to travel long distances to find work, or even move away altogether. Hastings, in East Sussex, is a busy seaside town. It has a lot of fascinating heritage to discover and plenty of tourist attractions, but during 1996 as many as one person in ten could not find any work.

Above This shopping street in the old part of Hastings is popular with tourists, but a brand-new shopping centre is being built, which will bring 1,000 new jobs to the area.

Left These fishermen's cottages in Hastings have been converted into fast-food restaurants.

New jobs

In some seaside towns, the local councils are trying to tackle these problems by helping to create new jobs. They are working hard to get money from the government, the European Community and from local businesses.

Above **This librarian is teaching a student computer skills which may help her to get a job.**

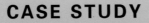

CASE STUDY

Rollerblading Coach

'Blade Marc' is a rollerblading coach on Hove seafront, in East Sussex. This is one of the best sites for blading in the world, including California, for its length, width and smoothness.

In-line skating, or blading, is a cross between roller-skating and ice-skating. Blade-skaters wear special boots fitted with four wheels in a line underneath. For safety, they also wear helmets, wrist guards, elbow pads and knee pads. But because blading is done on the pavement, once you have bought the equipment, skating is absolutely free! Rollerblading is the world's fastest-growing sport. It's great fun and anyone can do it.

'My youngest pupil is six and the oldest is seventy-five! Look out for blading at the 2000 Sydney Olympics!' says Marc.

Above **'Blade Marc' practises on Hove seafront.**

New service industries, such as banks and building societies, are being encouraged to set up in seaside towns. Towns such as Bournemouth, Blackpool and Brighton also have large conference centres for big meetings and concerts. These provide all-year-round employment for workers in offices, big hotels, restaurants, shops, even taxis!

Above **Bournemouth International Centre, where large organizations hold their conferences.**

Activity

When you go to the seaside, you are probably too busy having fun to notice the jobs people do. But if you look around carefully, you will probably see people working. Ask your family or friends to show you their seaside snapshots, and look at what is happening in the background. Can you see anybody working? Try making a collage of your own holiday photographs.

Left **A collage of holiday snaps taken on Brighton's Palace Pier.**

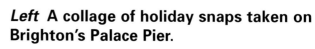

Although Brighton is still one of the most popular tourist towns in the country, only 11 per cent of the workforce have jobs in tourism. Banks and building societies employ 21 per cent of working people and 22 per cent work in shops and services.

More jobs are being created in Poole, in Dorset. New sports facilities are being developed, and the harbour is now an important centre for modern water sports, such as windsurfing and jet skiing. Luckily, local people do not just have to rely on tourism for work. There is also a busy commercial port and a passenger ferry to France. Today, Poole is one of the UK's fastest-growing seaside towns, creating new jobs and attracting more people to live there.

Boat owners in Poole offer tourists short trips around the harbour.

Seaside Schools

Seaside schools are as varied as seaside towns. If you look at their size, the number of pupils, the style of building or where they are built – no two seaside schools are exactly the same. What they do have in common is being on the coast.

The Mayflower County Primary School in Dovercourt, Harwich, takes its name from the Mayflower, the ship that took some of the first settlers to North America from Plymouth in 1620. One of its crew was John Smith, who lived in Harwich, and whose house still stands today.

Above A painting of the *Mayflower*.

Left The Mayflower School in Harwich was built in the 1930s and extended in the 1980s. This is the infant playground.

Going to the Carnival

Every year, King Offa Junior School in Bexhill-on-Sea in East Sussex, takes part in the town's Summer Carnival. This is the most colourful event of the year, when people take part in a procession, dressed up in fancy costumes and riding on decorated floats. People line up along the side of the road to watch the fun, and there are bands, clowns and a fun-fair. The event raises a lot of money for charity.

'In 1996, our float won the prize for "Best In Show" explains headteacher, Mr Thwaites. *'We all dressed up as Egyptians with long white costumes, and the float was decorated with hieroglyphs and pretend palm trees. I dressed up as the Pharoah!'*

Everyone from King Offa Junior School joined in to make their float really special.

The school makes many uses of its seaside position. The pupils often make trips to the beach to collect shells and fossils, and to investigate marine life. They also learn about the town's history by visiting the Maritime Museum and the Electric Palace Cinema. This cinema is one of the oldest in the country, built in 1911.

25

St Luke's Junior School, in Brighton, was built in 1903, high on a hill overlooking the sea. It is close to Queen's Park, which was built by a wealthy Victorian landowner next to his seaside villa. Today, it is still a popular place to relax, a few minutes' walk from the seafront. The pupils of St Luke's School investigate the park in many different ways in order to learn more about their local environment.

Above **St Luke's School is a tall, impressive building with a good view of the sea. It has many fine architectural features and is a listed building.**

Queen's Park has many typical Victorian features – large stone gateways, iron railings and a water fountain. The pupils make their own maps, showing the park's facilities, such as the bowling green and the duck pond.

Wherever they are built, schools are an important part of the wider community. Pupils usually live just a short bus ride or walk away, and their parents may have jobs in the same area.

Right **St Luke's is surrounded by Victorian terraced houses. On a field trip, pupils sketch the fancy wall mouldings built into the brickwork and the decorative balconies.**

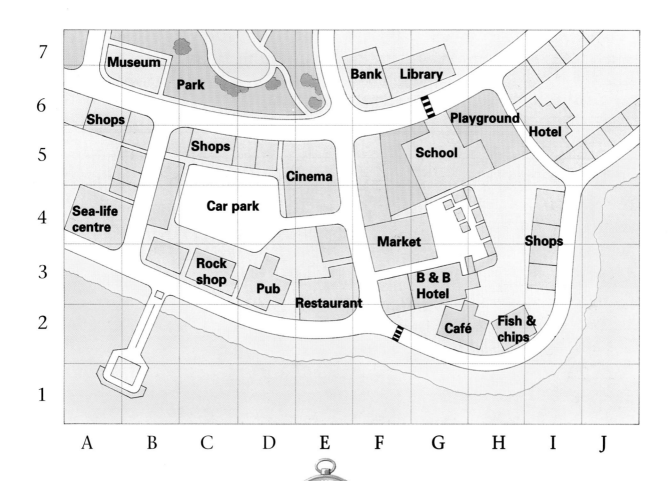

At special times of the year, many schools take part in local events. In Whitby, in North Yorkshire, the whole town takes part in the 'Blessing of the Boats' ceremony, which has been performed for centuries, praying for the safe return of fishing boats and lifeboats. These occasions are opportunities for people to get together and show that they are part of the same community.

Activity

On the map above, you will see all kinds of landmarks found in a seaside town. The co-ordinate for the rock shop is C3. Can you work out the co-ordinates for the 'bed and breakfast' hotel, fish and chip shop, zebra crossings, park and school? Why not try designing a grid map of where you live, showing one of your favourite walks, and the things you see along the way?

On the Move

All seaside towns need good transport and communication links to grow and thrive, as they have to cope with large numbers of visitors as well as the resident population.

Seaside ports

Many of today's seaside towns are old sea ports, which were once the main ways of entering and leaving the country. After the Industrial Revolution, most shipping used the great city ports, such as London, Liverpool and Belfast. Today, smaller sea ports and towns still carry goods and passengers across the Channel.

In Folkestone, in Kent, the new Channel Tunnel provides a fast link with France for cars, lorries coaches and trains, taking only 35 minutes.

The Wight Link ferry service, between the Isle of Wight and the UK mainland, is a vital link for the local people, bringing in food supplies as well as tourists.

Southwold Lighthouse

Lighthouses are well-known landmarks in many seaside towns, flashing a light out to sea to guide ships round the coast. Each lighthouse has its own pattern of flashing lights which marks it out from the others.

Southwold is a seaside town in Suffolk. Its lighthouse was built in 1886 right on the seafront. The brilliant white tower is 31 metres high and has a spiral staircase with 99 steps up to the lantern room.

Keith Seaman, the lighthouse attendant, does not have to live at the lighthouse, but he does have to look after the equipment. He also takes school parties on tours of the tower. The lantern used to be kept alight by oil pumped up from the basement by hand. Nowadays, it is powered by electricity and controlled by a computer.

'The light can be seen as far as 35 km out to sea, and it is as bright as 47,000 candles!' says Keith.

Right **Inside the top of the lighthouse, Keith keeps a regular check on the equipment.**

Above **Southwold's lighthouse can be seen from every part of the town.**

Above The Great Northern Railway's poster of 'The Jolly Fisherman'.

The Railway Age

Some of the UK's oldest seaside resorts are on coastlines close to big cities. After the introduction of the railways, these resorts became popular because they were only a short ride away.

When the railways were first run by electricity in the 1920s and 1930s, seaside towns became even easier to reach. Different railway companies tried to attract passengers using colourful posters with cheerful seaside characters. The Great Northern Railway promoted Skegness with 'The Jolly Fisherman', who is still part of the town's logo today.

Above The traffic problem in Brighton, in East Sussex has been helped by a Park-and-Ride scheme.

Activity

The flow of traffic in settlements can be measured to show the busiest times of the day and of the year. Try carrying out your own traffic-flow survey by recording the number of cars passing by a given spot. Carry out the survey at busy times and quiet times, and compare the results. Remember that roads are dangerous places. Take an adult with you, always stay on the pavement and keep a safe distance from cars.

Solving traffic problems

Nowadays, more people travel by car than train. Seaside planners are trying to cope with the extra cars by encouraging motorists to use different routes to get to the town. Park-and-Ride schemes in some towns allow motorists to leave their cars on the outskirts of town and travel to the town centre by bus.

Seaside vehicles

In a seaside town, you will notice some unusual types of transport. Open-top buses allow tourists see a town's main attractions. There are also funicular railways and trams. The world's first electric tramway opened in Blackpool in 1885, and 18.5 kilometres of track are still used. In towns built on estuaries, such as Poole, local ferry services are used by local people and tourists.

A horse-drawn tram in the seaside town of Douglas, on the Isle of Man.

31

Shopping and Entertainment

The first thing you notice when you start exploring a seaside town is the number of different entertainment and leisure facilities. Swimming, sunbathing, exploring rock pools and playing on the beach are all important parts of a seaside holiday. Donkey rides on the beach, Punch and Judy shows and 'pitch and putt' golf are still popular. There are also more modern attractions, such as heritage centres and 'tropical' indoor swimming complexes.

Shops and restaurants

Most people like shopping for souvenirs when they are on holiday. You can find shops along most seafronts selling buckets and spades and ornaments covered in shells. Other shops sell local crafts and antiques. Seaside towns usually have a wide choice of restaurants. Beach stalls sell cockles and mussels, and ice-creams and candy floss are also part of a visit to the seaside.

Donkey rides on Skegness beach are part of a fun day out.

Things to see and do

Piers are popular landmarks in many seaside towns. They are only found in England and Wales. Over 100 piers were built during Victorian and Edwardian times, using fancy cast iron and wood. Today, only fifty remain, and many are listed buildings, which means they cannot be pulled down. Piers are places for traditional seaside pastimes, such as eating fish and chips, and enjoying amusement arcades and helter-skelter rides. To show how important piers are, 1996 was marked the 'Year of the Pier'.

Above Many seaside towns have their own fun-fair, which is open all year round.

Southend Pier in Essex is the longest pier in the UK and measures 3.4 km, while Brighton's Palace Pier is one of the busiest, visited by over 3.5 million people every year.

Left Stalls selling sticks of rock and other sweets are often found on piers.

33

Over the past thirty years, seaside towns in the UK have had to compete with foreign resorts. Many people now travel to warmer countries. Seaside towns in the UK have had to improve their tourist facilities. On the west coast of Scotland, the seaside towns of Ayr, Troon, Prestwick and Girvan are already well known for their safe, sandy beaches, but now this popular resort area also has Wonderwest World – a multi-million-pound leisure complex with swimming pools, a fun-fair and sports facilities.

Above Sea-life centres are popular whatever the weather.

Activity

Almost everyone buys postcards when they visit the seaside. They show many popular features of the town, and make good souvenirs. Design a postcard of your own town, village or suburb, showing which you think are its most attractive features.

Right A souvenir shop in Perranporth, Cornwall.

Tourism all year round

There are often many places in a seaside town to visit all year round. There are maritime museums in many seaside towns. Local heritage – the history, arts and natural beauty of a town – is also being promoted to attract visitors.

The old fishing town of Whitby, in North Yorkshire, is in an area called the 'Heritage Coast', and holidaymakers are encouraged to visit the historic sites along this coast. The beautiful North York Moors run right up to the town, and there is even something for Dracula fans! The author, of *Dracula*, Bram Stoker, set many of his famous stories in Whitby, and visitors can take a special tour of the town, accompanied by a Dracula lookalike.

A view of Whitby, showing the historic clifftop Abbey in the background.

Sports

Surfing, windsurfing, body-boarding and sailing are some of the water sports you can do in seaside towns. Certain areas of the coast in Devon and Cornwall are known as 'surfers' paradise'. You can also hire boats for sea fishing and scuba diving. Seaside towns are often chosen to stage world-famous sporting events. St Andrews, in Scotland, hosts international golf tournaments, and Douglas, on the Isle of Man, attracts thousands of visitors for the annual TT Motorcycle Race.

Above **A surfer rides the waves at Newquay, in Cornwall.**

Where do people stay?

Large seaside resorts, such as Scarborough in Yorkshire, still attract over a million visitors a year. But Blackpool has 16.5 million visitors a year! Some stay in 'bed and breakfasts', others may camp or stay in caravans, holiday cottages, holiday camps or hotels.

Right **Holiday camps provide special entertainers and a lot of different things to do.**

Blackpool Pleasure Beach and Tower

Blackpool Pleasure Beach is the UK's most popular free tourist attraction. Over 7.2 million people visit it each year. It has the world's tallest and fastest roller-coaster, known as 'Pepsi Max – the Big One'. It is 71 metres high and can reach speeds of nearly 140 kph!

The New Big Wheel was built in 1990 and can carry 216 passengers. If the Wheel stops while you are in the top carriage, you are more than 32 metres high in the air. The five wooden roller-coasters travel the equivalent of ten times around the world each season, and visitors to the Pleasure Beach eat over 75 kilometres of hot dogs end to end!

The Blackpool Tower was built in 1894. It is over 158 metres high. There are two lifts to the top of the tower, where you can post your postcards to friends at home. At the base of the Tower, there is a huge building with an Undersea World Centre and the Tower Dungeon.

Above Blackpool Sands, with the famous Tower in the background. The Tower is over 100 years old.

Right Donkey rides are fun. Nowadays the donkeys' health must be checked regularly by a vet.

Planning for the Future

Seaside towns need to plan for the future – to increase employment for the resident population and improve facilities for visitors. Town planners are now developing attractions that will last all year round. Yet it is important that the beautiful natural environment of seaside areas is also protected.

The European Community set up the COAST project (Co-ordinated Action for Seaside Towns) in 1992, and has members from many European countries, including Italy, France, Greece and Spain. The project looks at ways of regenerating seaside towns, by setting up small- and medium-sized businesses to provide better-paid employment.

Millions of people go on coastal walks each year. Too many visitors can lead to the erosion of the land.

The housing needs of seaside towns are changing. Census information from the last twenty years shows that more young people live in seaside towns today, so there is a need for housing suitable for single people. Money needs to be invested in low-cost homes for families, not just in luxury flats and retirement homes.

Like all land, the coast is under constant attack from the weather. Natural erosion from the wind, rain, snow, and the sea itself, takes its toll on the UK's coastline. The cliffs south of Bridlington, on England's east coast, are being eroded by the sea at a rate of two metres a year.

The cliffs at West Runton in Norfolk are protected from the sea by wooden sea defences which stop them from being eroded.

More work is now being done to care for the natural environment of coastal settlements. 'Enterprise Neptune' is the National Trust's longest and most successful campaign to help protect the coastline. The Trust has succeeded in buying one-sixth of the coastline around the UK. The aim is to protect these areas from erosion and new development.

Government money has made this bird colony in Northumberland a safe place for cormorants, gannets and gulls.

Pollution

One of the major causes of pollution is human waste. In the UK, 13.5 hundred million litres of untreated waste are still pumped into the sea every day. It is dangerous to swimmers and windsurfers, who can become ill from swallowing the water. Industrial and agricultural waste pollutes the sea as well, but new laws are forcing businesses to treat their waste products before dumping them.

With the help of new laws and a promise to spend £1 billion to improve bathing waters, many beaches are now cleaner, but much more needs to be done.

The Seaside Awards, co-ordinated by the Tidy Britain Group, first started in 1992, and The European Blue Flag Awards encourage seaside towns to tackle the pollution problem. In 1995, over 130 resort beaches were tested and fifty had clean enough water, with thirty-one being awarded the full 'Blue Flag Award'.

CASE STUDY

Sandown Bay Protesters

On 8 May 1996, the residents of Sandown Bay, on the Isle of Wight, felt they could take no more. With banners waving, more than 400 men, women and children, including councillors and members of pressure groups marched to Sandown Pier. They were protesting against a proposal to pump all the island's partially-treated sewage through Sandown Bay.

The water company was prepared to lengthen the sewage pipe into the sea by 3 km, but refused to introduce extra disinfection methods that would guarantee clean beaches and bathing water.

'We can put a man on the moon... so why can't we keep raw sewage out of the sea?' asked one marcher.

The children of Broadlea Primary School gave their support by singing songs and making banners.

A young protester makes her case for improving the environment!

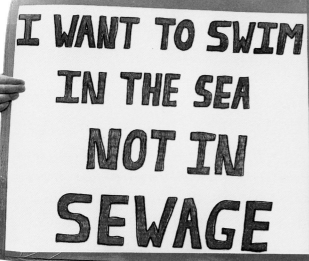

I WANT TO SWIM IN THE SEA NOT IN SEWAGE

How to Investigate a Seaside Town

There are many ways to start investigating a seaside town. Below are some ideas for you to consider as starting points for your research.

First-hand information

Many seaside resorts have their own tourist information brochures and leaflets. These are filled with lists of places to visit and will help you to find out about popular features and well-known landmarks. The local newspapers include interesting news items about daily life in a seaside town. The letters page will show you what people think about proposed changes and future plans for the area. National newspapers, magazines and television programmes also have features on tourism and environmental problems.

People in the know

Your local library can provide all kinds of information about seaside towns. The reference section is particularly useful. The librarian will help you to find census information, Ordnance Survey maps, books, encyclopaedias, magazines and newspapers.

The Planning Department of the local Council can send you information about future plans for the area, along with facts and figures. They may also have a special Education Officer, who can help you with this kind of research. To find out where to begin, try the council's Public Relations Office. The nearest County Record Office will have old records and maps showing how a settlement has changed over the years.

Maps

There are a variety of maps to look at when studying a seaside town. A road atlas will show you where to find it in the UK, but you will need a larger-scale map, such as an Ordnance Survey map, to see it in detail.

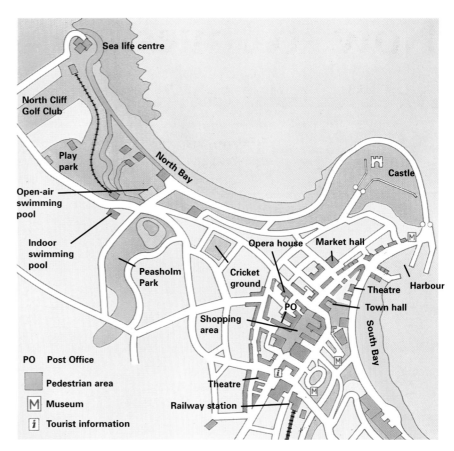

Census information

Census information shows us how particular areas have changed over the years, and what they are like now. The information includes the number of people living in an area and their ages, whether they are single, married or divorced, where they were born, whether they are working, unemployed or retired, what kind of housing they live in and whether or not they own a car. You can find census information in any large public library.

Places to visit

Maritime museums, heritage centres, sea-life centres and tourist information offices.

Collecting and presenting your evidence

Collect all the information you find, such as leaflets, bus or train tickets, museum guides, postcards and newspaper cuttings, and design your own seaside scrapbook or poster promoting the area. Think about using other types of media, such as CD-ROM encyclopaedias, photographs or tape recordings of interviews. Also, if you have access to a computer, you could enter your findings on a database.

Notes About this Book

The main text in each book in the Landmarks series provides general information about four types of settlement within the contexts of communities, work, schools, transport, shopping and entertainment, and change. Each book in the series features the same areas of study so that the four different types of settlements can be compared easily with each other within a general context.

Case studies give specific information about a particular aspect of each chapter and sometimes provide direct quotes from people who live and work in different kinds of settlements. Children can use this information to make a direct comparison with their own experience.

The activities are designed so that children from any type of settlement can do them. They can be used to demonstrate what the main text has already stated about the locality mentioned in the book, or as a contrast. Throughout the series children are encouraged to work with the various tools that a geographer uses to study a particular area, such as mapping and graph skills, conducting surveys and using primary source evidence such as census material.

What is a Seaside Town? (pages 4–7)
This chapter gives a brief outline of the different types of seaside towns found in the UK. The language and examples have been designed to encourage children to look around them, and either compare or contrast their own settlement with that of a seaside town. The text examines what special features distinguish seaside towns from other types of settlement.

Activity on page 7:
This activity is designed to illustrate how to use a map to extract information about local landmarks. Encourage the children to think about where the various attractions are on the map, so that they can plan an easy route for each day without having to go too far.

People and Communities (pages 8–15)
This chapter investigates the kinds of people living in a seaside town, its key buildings and focal points of seaside life. The chapter encourages children to compare their own experiences with those in the text.

Activity on page 15:
This activity encourages children to think about the advantages and disadvantages of where they live. Ask them why they feel that some aspects are advantageous and others are not. Are there often bad weather conditions? Do the children live too far from shops and services? Are there plenty of things for them to do? Can the children think of any improvements they would like to make to their local area?

Earning a Living (pages 16–23)
This chapter deals with the seaside town economy, what kinds of jobs people do and how this has changed in recent years. Children are encouraged to think about how the nature of a seaside settlement influences the types of employment found there.

Activity on page 22:
This activity encourages children to use their own primary source evidence to explore the nature of work in a seaside town. Ask the children to think about what happens to these jobs during the winter. Is all the work seasonal work? Can the children find any examples of jobs that people do all year round?

Seaside Schools (24–27)
In this chapter children are encouraged to compare or contrast their school and its surrounding area with seaside examples illustrated in the text.

Activity on page 27:
This mapping activity encourages children to use grid references to find landmarks on a map. The exercise also stimulates the children to produce a grid map of their own. You can try this exercise for the area around the school. Find an aerial photograph of your locality and lay a tracing-paper grid over it. Ask children to find various familiar places on the map and describe their position as grid references.

On the Move (pages 28–31)
This chapter encourages children to think about the importance of good transport networks in and around seaside towns, and the environmental implications of modern forms of transport. Children are also encouraged to notice the more unusual forms of transport provided for tourists.

Activity on page 30:
Children are encouraged to think about the amount of traffic on the UK's roads. They can break down their survey into different types of transport and numbers counted. Input the results into a spread sheet on a computer.

Shopping and Entertainment (pages 32–37)
This chapter shows how the character of a seaside town is reflected in the local shops and facilities found there, and how these are changing.

Activity on page 34:
This activity encourages children to focus on the good points about where they live, and what might make it attractive to visitors. Produce a classroom display illustrating all the features that the children like about their own area.

Change and the Future: (pages 38–41)
This chapter shows that whilst seaside settlements are attractive places to live, the changing way of life can bring problems, which need to be resolved.

Glossary

Census A survey which is carried out every ten years in the UK, to find out how many people live in an area, where they live and their way of life.

Chambermaid A hotel worker who makes the beds and cleans the rooms.

Crescent A street of houses shaped in a semi-circle.

Erosion The action of weather, water, ice and wind, leading to rocks and other materials wearing away and breaking down.

Estuary The part of a river which runs into the sea.

European Community A group of countries in Europe that has agreed to work together to improve their economies and way of life.

Funicular A railway that goes up a steep hillside or cliff.

Headland A narrow strip of land running out into the sea.

Income The money that people have to live on.

Industrial Revolution The time during the eighteenth and early nineteenth centuries when the development of new machinery led to the growth of factories in the UK.

Invest To place money in a new building development, factory or business in the hope of making a profit at a later date.

Listed building A building of special interest which is protected from unnecessary change by the local council.

Logo A symbol which makes something easy to recognize, for example, the little Wayland man at the front of this book.

National Trust An organization which looks after buildings of historic importance and land that is under threat.

Planners People who make plans for the development of an area.

Promenade A wide walkway that is next to a seafront.

Redundant When a worker is not needed any longer by an employer.

Regency The period 1811–1820, before the Prince Regent became King George IV.

Regenerate To improve the life of a town with the help of new investment.

Skipper The captain of a boat.

Terrace A row of houses joined together.

Victorian The period of Queen Victoria's reign from 1837–1901.